P6   G9
  67

ALKALI

M000316486

Craig Dworkin

COUNTERPATH

DENVER

2015

A L K A L I

Counterpath

Denver, Colorado

www.counterpathpress.org

Printed in the United States of America

Library of Congress Cataloging-in-Publication Data

Dworkin, Craig Douglas
[Poems. Selections]
  Alkali / Craig Dworkin.
    pages   cm
  Includes bibliographical references.
  ISBN 978-1-933996-47-9 (softcover : acid-free paper)
  I. Title.
PS3604.W66A6 2015
811'.6—dc23

                                        2014034836

CONTENTS

ACKNOWLEDGMENTS   *vii*

IN THE DARK WOOD   I

FELDSPAR   17

THE CRYSTAL TEXT   25

HALIGRAPHY   43

ALL SAINTS   67

THE FALLS   71

NOTES AND SOURCES   117

ACKNOWLEDGMENTS

Profound gratitude and warm thanks to Julie Carr and Tim Roberts at Counterpath, the entire crew at the Book Arts Studio in the Marriott Library, Michael Cross at Compline Press, Mónica de la Torre at *BOMB*, Marjorie Perloff, and Danny Snelson with *Poetry & Poetics*.

ALKALI

IN THE DARK WOOD /
/ *NELLA SELVA OSCURA*

in the (it)

in the (fem)

imine ylides
indium, indigane

ennead

a knell (*la glas*), an echo of—

a nail (*un clou*)

    struck, aglow, annealing

an arc, an ache,

        and then —

the stand of boughs on farther march

              in annuent ascent

La vie — n'est-elle pas organisation avec sentiment?

pebbled seeds accede to trees' rings wrung
from ripples fixed in lignid lines

annual, annulate

the acetate of Ariel's cry —
petrified, revenant, dissipating — static
addenda on a dendral record
of concentric nested tremors

glistening and resinous

across a knoll: the whole, in rounds, repealing

Who hears the sound in the dark wood damping?

to hear
in the (her)

of what inheres, inured,
innate in names (in yours)

aire over signature in Lawes

skin saporous with salt, lashes matted over eyes

a succulent spray splays over sand — so named
because the ashe of it serve to make glas with

defined as any compound containing the group NH

null law
no loss

leaving wind, in riot, ramified along the lawn

a little pod, lavished

parfum a la vanille
elle nie la fane, par fume

the scent of soap on skin we do not know

Everything, entheat, happens exactly as it must.

Running of foldage in the margent of the pannels. . . .
    —*Jrnl. of the Derbyshire Arch. Soc.* III: 33 (1703)

Fold grown feldspar in spathe fields sprat pleats failing to pare.

Over march of path: fault of fulled runs filtered by spare yielding spart spats; sprattle of foliage and felt fall to sparging to fill a scaf.

Over path — fulled filtered yielding spats of foliage fall to to fill.

March of fault of runs by spare spart sprattle of felt sparging a scaf.

Fold over march of grown path — fault of feldspar fulled runs in spathe filtered by spare fields yielding spart — sprat spats sprattle pleats of foliage and felt, failing to fall to sparging pare to fill a scaf.

Fold over grown path — feldspar fulled in spathe filtered fields
yielding sprat spats — pleats of foliage failing to fall to pare to fill.

THE CRYSTAL TEXT

(after Clark Coolidge)

The moment at which a text or depiction reaches out most irresistibly to a thing seen or expressed is also the moment at which it mobilizes the accidents and duplicities of markmaking most flagrantly, most outlandishly — all in the service of pointing through them, and somehow with them, to another body that is their guarantor.

—T. J. Clark

A rose quartz quarters on my desk. It obligates. It obliquates. Around an axis the crystal twists. The crystal finds an assectation in this text. The rock assesses — and corrects. Smoothing from the cut a curve of surface caresses and assents. It stays assayed. Any true bequesting must remain unsaid. The crystal is oblique. The crystal was obliged. It is expressive, biomorphic and easily anthropomorphized, and yet, at the same time, the most remote and indifferent to human wishes... the most like a body the least like an organism. It is always more important, more interesting, more capable (full of rights): it has no duty to me whatsoever. The tone is fading imperceptibly as I watch. Its opalescence spreads with the color's obsolescence. A rock is a clock. It marks; it keeps; it bides; it takes. It weighs like something else on her mind, but it can wait. Skin's elasticity calibrates a kind of long-term dermal chronologue. Impurities in the massive material fibre the fleshy hue. The rock's muscle relaxes. Edges distress the desk. A rock lasts, clastic. The crystal scrawls where the base has scraped the laminate. The rose leaves lesions along the plastic plate. The quartz abrades. It banns. It banks. The stone upbraids me when I look away. The rose abates. The stone projects. The top counters. Each cleave desperates the hopes of cohesion. Nearing close, the cliff looks treacherous and steep. The crystal stalls. The rock is rested, completely intensiled, intense. The larger wall palls; the composites disparate. Some pockets hollow when the gravel falls. At last the local clasp collapses. Two sides wrinkle like a ball of crumpled paper. The rock swivels, thick-wristed in its partial pivot. The crystal bevels against the level and plumbs. The crystal riddles. Ridges nick. White streaks striate the flank like nail marks. The cirrus thins. The crystal clouds. It casts. A rock includes. Lamina flake like keratin from the glassy margarite. Nacre under lacquer suspends. Salmon settles to a turbid fathom. The rose doles, saturated to a depth. A rose arises from titanian traces. Before it rights the rose twists sinistrous. The crystal faults. Some helicities of salt cause a delirium. The crystal is lit. The crystal is limned. Planes grade against the rim like an angle of sinking. Waves rock. Rocks log, and list. The crystal tilts and skews. Some soft-stalked rose takes on, and sizes. It whelms and tanks. It fails to avoid. The hull of a rock lies heavy in the silt. Our horizon slews. Larger structures suffer with a catastrophic loss. Conchoidal fractures spread from impact like ripples from a stone dropped into water. Arrayed, concentric, the ocean's repetitions rame; its heaves, sorry, endlessly vent. Dry land looms as a *memento mare*. From tailings' piles quartz accrues.

The lonely stone strips ply from ply. Wreathing wave upon wave, light lattices on water. Laced oscillants plait as the nascent pleats, implacid, pleach, reach out and overlay. Reflectance decks. Crestings braid the ceaseless weaving of uneven waves. Surges hail from the air; tides allide the coast; each swell chills the surf as it leaves; the sea sieves the sand to sift the silted slurry's lees. Strands lather. A rim clouds. Troughs roughen. A surface reeves. A backwash reparates the beach's polish. Lustrant saline depurates the rock. Rounded pebbles roke. A quartz is always centered. Electrons spin with angular momenta; their charges quantize. Quartz enlarges. Somewhere rock is washed in salts. A crystal cleanses. The dust breeds. Molecules waltz and halt. Minerals spirit. Volatiles solve. Vibrations ratio. Vibrant sympathies incide. The crystal oscillates at a frequency I feel but cannot see. Standing waves resonate and cancel. Sinical light casts a clinical glare. The rock is loud, though it resounds too low for me to hear. The crystal is slow. A crystal is frequent. I think of it tuning as it turns. The crystal can only transmit, but no one is listening. The stone insists but is never urgent. A rose encodes. The crystal quills. It evinces a will to formation, and the impossibility of forming *any other way*. The court's report demands its deposition. The discourse of the quartz records soliloquies of ice, speaking ceaselessly of the beauty of its own snows. A certain curtain ascertains. Folds drape like glaciated crinoline with a glycerined sheen. The silken swikes. It rises to the light. The passerine weeps at each appearance. Sun swipes at the rose in passing sweeps. Mica glints. Phases shift across gaunt ellipses. Shade swerves. Shadows circle the base in a sciatic sway. Their shapes, for a moment, leave Lissajous curves. The desk serves as an oscilloscopic screen, picturing the frequency of unheard solar sounds. Filaments in interference elongate, slake, foreshortening, and fade. The crystal is a lens. The crystal lends. It colors. The crystal as a prism imprisons certain shades. Its polar optics set selective spectra free. It smoothes so you may play. A sinusoidal period repeats. Curtained apertures curtail the erasures from halation that might whiten out the frame. Lassed wind slats the window-glass. The shade staggers, wobbles and rocks. Acclivous clouds in their upward slope attenuate, contrailing. Through a half-drawn sash the rose is stoked; the tawny rokes remember in a flash; the crystal surprises the vestal sunrise. The crystal's photographs cycle daily. Fuscal purples temper while the festal blushes rise. Its silicate thresholds in the dusk. Their pairs share oxygen. The silicon is still again, its bands akin to holding hands. Iron impurities profess a kind of faith. They stipple the base. The rock's stenography courts a short reporting. Sodium chloride in its halide cubes keeps well allied with quartz. The rose, immobile, corresponds. Molecules resile and collide. Structures rebuke forms. Stones sink and rise, through the magma and the crust; they melt and then grow cold. The crystal glances. The crystal glaces. Up close one can see a crease in the crystal where it seems to fold: an erotics of the rock. Rust spots macle on the bottom block. The rose, arroused, glistens. The crystal winks and lustres. It sheens where it has not been sheared and underneath the fingers feels slick. The rock absorbs the oils from my hands. Out of the cool the crystal's surface sweats. The crystal films. The skin thins. The crystal crafts occasions. The rose proposes new arrangements. My placement is assigned. Deficiencies in the grid split chips to sand. The crystal is a siren. The crystal is a sign. The crystal sings, refrains, reprises. The rungs of its lattice ring in rounds. Phonoliths lithe the silence like a cipher. A tone lires the aire. The rock rinks when I knock it. The block proves strong; its brink assays, stays hale and sound. Stimulated, in circles, the stone sings its synchronous song. At the centre of the rose, its secret: an absence; the delicate folded structures cup nothing with such care. I have limited myself here to the crystal, to everything among the missing. The rose is the moment toward which everything is drawn. In its reflection, the crystal is a twin, split between my eyes. In the waning light the stone looks wan. The rock intrudes. Each block was composite. The crust quenches. Trenches thrust. Feldspar sponges and pumices the granite. A stratum plunges. The valley summons. Fieldstones, among alpine flowers, lie. Asteraceæ bloom above the buried gems.

Covered with clay, capacious stones forget, delight, make glad, avert dismay. Stems weave a hurdle. Eathers stake. *Les pierres précieuses s'enfouissant.* Beneath the road: the beach. Gravel skirts from erosion expose. Micæ brighten. Fissures lode. Vents distain their distal facies. Strata fold. Crystals clear the surface with a soiled breach. A rose eclodes. Precessions of crystals uncover vistal ambits. Glaces glare. The rose imbues. A clear-cut leam lingers and scows. A scream plows itself. Crisis pews. Rust tones, imbrues and braces. This poem writes on a bleached sheet of just such water-logged stone. The quartz fashions a nappe around its axis. The crystal taches quickly from the friction. This poem rights; the stone upends; the poem appends. Each against the other stites. A rock is a fraction of some other stone. Nitrides mask the etchants. Each crystal was embedded. The roche once was rached. Each face is false —

irregular, inconstant. The rock is just. The rose aches. The cusp is hastate in its jut. A ridge knaps from the back of the neck, where it tapers to a wedge. A clutch of quartzes gestate as they hutch. Accretions seek the furthest edge. The stone is asleep, but not for long. The rose will not take. The quartz, when I clasp it, forges a tache. The stocked rock squares like a fist. It holds fast. It fastens. It fits. In the end, its commitments leave me so undone. The stone deprives. It quits. Lives quiet. Each crystal remembers the history of its seeds. A bud remembers its limb. The viewer forgets his task. The crystal is sincere. Its sinuate facets pare. I stare at the crystal daily, dutifully. Cut stone fascinates. The crystal is a die. The crystal decides. It flushes and ashes. In a flash the reflection ushers in the dusk. The crystal text, diurnal, reflects. The crystal cannot die. Still, the stone sits there. The crystal is couched. Its skill facets skew.

The rose arrests. It vouches and attests. Sincipital wedges brow the crown. The rose quartz functions as a skull — a *memento mori* immobile on my desk. Miners cull the gravel for the gems. Crystalline does not mean *dead*. A *vanitas* reminds. Some single form reduplicates; layers tile; coverings cleave; the shingle shells clean out. A rock is a reliquary of structure. The lapidary cerns. The klaprothite weathers. The rose relinquishes and binds, leaving loans behind. Dilapidated kerns lack bite. Quartz earns its salary form. The stone scuttles, and scuttles the shallow crest. Valéry's storm stirs the waves of the sea. Rocks impinge upon the loam. A gem emerges from the scree. The crystal percusses. It settles. It scores. Stones in soil immerse. The crystal misses its bed. It saddles. It ettles itself. As the water lets go of its solutes stone sublimes and the crystals grow. Window-glass flows slowly down. Lachryma lapse with time. The rose is complicit in the processes. Any given donative cannot be resolute. A fragile crystal fractures. Quartz chips scales from the cliff. Tissues fissure. The issue ceases. A tear refracts the light to blind. With a pause across the tristal crest, it passes down along the cheek — and checks. The crystal for a moment cannot be seen. But, since the crystal itself is colorless, what we perceive when we look at it is the color and structure of the rose and not the crystal itself. This crystal as I count is a tristetrahedron. Its plicatures increase. Its pleas protect. Some stone provects. We construe the beauty of the rose from its imperfections, its failures. A grid ranges, and will continue until something gets in its way. This quartz is generous. A quartz is generative. Its growth is thwarted by the given depositions. A lattice by additions accretes. The crystal assists. The crystal encysts. This crystal is discrete. Its xenophobic structure is

allergic to the stranger. The crystal is dedicated. It is given
to the word. The crystal is addicting. The terms decline; the
stone hands over; the beholder deposes. The rock mocks. It
scolds. It says to me, again and again, and I cannot help it: you
are devoted; you have betrayed; you have been consecrated;
you have been delivered. Something has gotten in my way.
A foiled flectance tains. This rock once was cleft. It now is
balanced, like a heart, to the left. The crystal is motionless
when I write on it. The heart abstracts itself. The crystal
obliterates. This rock once was rifted. The crystal is sits. This
crystal seems uprighted when placed on its thinnest face. Sawn
boards delineate the borders of the profile's raw drawn dorn.
Adjacent sides appear uneven from above. Coved edges blunt.
This crystal would be dorsal if it were a blade. The rose makes
its presence felt. It gives time, times and takes. The rock was

oblated. It obviates all debts. The crystal was a gift, and so it should suspend the present — holding open a space that can only await: a delay in quartz (as one might say "a poem in prose"). The crystal's commissures craft raphes. Facets afaite. Until the moment it was seen it seemed to be agraphic. A rose shows a continuous multiplication with identity. The geometry of rocks reforms. The back of the face is oblate. Its cropping corners must have been pared. The rock leafs. The rose laments. A focal conic generates a quadric. Tiers factor. Quartz stems. Parallel aments range with changeful poses. Petals ravel. The rental pends. The crystal as a gift forecloses most exchanges. The crystal stipulates and will not bargain. It refuses to edit its obligatory rates of interest and estrangement. The crystal scries a small circle in scratches. Its benefactor, a signatory, credits and ascribes. The crystal chooses. Seeds propagate to shoots. Scales scar and stipule. Edges ripple and dent. The crystal is a scribe. Its pumicing scumbles the imitation grain. Rain pummels the clay; it pocks and washes. The rose will not come clean. In the plot I write the path of the rock is sinuous. Gravel marks the border of the lot. The crystal is oblivious, intransitive. It causes me to waver. Its planed arrangements stagger. Lids occlude in droop as the recludent muscles flag. Periorbitals bolden. The crystal is duplicitous. It clears and confines; throws open and thwarts — *vighnakarta, vighnaharta* — the quartz removes obstacles; the stone obstructs; it locks out — shuts in. The stone recludes. The rose is holden. The crystal does nothing to everything. It refuses to object. I try to bestow the stone; it hands right back. It remains a gift. The crystal's indifference makes me wistful. The rock is constant. This crystal is my proof. Only it can know how accurate and imprecise I have been here — the extents of my unfaithfulness and simultaneous fidelities. The rosary beads with polished stones. A prose concedes its meter. The bank, in cycles, rents. An airy cirrus rises where the stream is prone to speed; it streaks the shrinking daylight, pinks and patterns like the strata of the stone. Beyond the pane the branches bar the darkling with their arch and sweep. The crystal damps. The quench tapers. The rose quartz quells. A luminance is almost spent. The sunset steeps; the crystal dyes the passing brightness. The glow grows lambent; the balance of the lamber shadows; it goldens as it goes. The rock is out of time. The crystal was beheld. The crystal is beholden.

Turning sharply toward the setting sun, an elegant
shadow diminishes.

The sounds of the rusting wind startled the roosting
bird.

— Chao Shao-an

Tout évolue aussi vers une parfaite sécheresse.

—Francis Ponge

Alkali like ice accretes across the rocks' lips; slopes
suspend the sundered boulders in repose.

Halation at the lake's horizon occasions the visual collision of the distant hills; they granulate behind a scrim of calinated haze.

Some pinnacled salts maze with manacled molecules; chlorides, in fragile shackles, concatenate; traceries of natric lattices encase the pan in lace.

Selenites precipitate from brine sheets, each prepared
as parchment by the wind with steady sandings waged
against indentures on their brittle skins.

Pollen spores intoxicate and flake like powdered ore to stain the eyelids; streaks of beautiful black soda-ash check in their caliginous runs.

Bleached caliche grades to silt; baked alluvials layer
with a gravelly loam; a trace of raspite wrests through
rifted strata, rusting to the west.

From a bluff beyond the range of water shaling at the shore: the straight line of a causeway lost to shimmer; tufts of gramma curling like acanthus as they seed; celandine in slow invasion; helianthus quailing, daily, in a rattling disarray.

Beneath a belt of sheet-basalt and granite cap: assault of heat in welter on the east slot wall.

Chalk Creek chokes with seed downstream from cottonwood and willow; the populous riparians parade along in tributary march.

Here, their aments without calyx or corolla blister in aridity; cells crenate from lysis with a desiccating flush; winds astringe, eliciting the same saliva that they then contemn.

A few thin clouds abrade the Alice blue; the chalice of
the Great Lake's basin salinates in an evaporative slake;
sky, draining, etiolates; haze shades to hazard the
azure's hue.

As swallows sallow in the shallow light, their shadows cause cælifera to skew in sudden stridulating flights.

Recalcitrance pitches paltering lances; bodies broach obliquely to — then right; sected shadows angle at the sloped approach; hinged limbs flect and square, *une fausse équerre*, to trace a chitinous cousin to the compass as they fold.

Audible above a brace of lithic plinths the shale stylobate resounds the crepitations of its stone foundation cooling in the dusk.

With the spine thrown forward in a concave arc,
secretions arroused from spiracles accresce above the
coccyx; the droplets bead, quaver with the thrust, and
pool to lave — seasoning the skin with a salacious taste.

The house where I live, my life, what I write: I dream that all that might appear from far off like these cubes of rock salt look close up.

Emotions result from some felicities of salts; lysine
bridges span sodium channels with a glycosylated clasp;
ligands rax out and collapse; ions cross capillated space
in a delirious embrace — halides precessing in reprise
— and we feel the reeling in turn.

With a fissured script of networked rifts, divisions on a ground record the spread of tears across the bed; the hirst rises and dries; lacunar craquelures craze lamina like a lacquered glaze.

Alkali halides glare the haze.

Accruals of shadow under boulder-curves merge; margins abrupt, abut, then mute and smooth; night air rarefies to dissipate the smother it cannot abide; and for a while, everything radiates, cools and quickens.

Slow, slow, fresh fount, keepe time, for selde it is that
love alloweth us to weep: deposits celebrate despite
their burn and sting; foam resides — the granulating
spume, in turn; verses calibrate their cumulative rates;
elegies resign from love poems that have learned to face
their fate.

ALL SAINTS

Weepe you no more, sad fountains.

—John Dowland

I.

Ored arches ern
inky rivers out
rust-raddled rows
ranged even over
aging riven rove-
ringed axes — randed
ewers raining ash,
raked eye ruts uttering reams.

II.

Eves addle ere
our ender annum
ages airs rung
under riper eaves.

THE FALLS

Étrangement et singulièrement j'ai aimé tout
ce qui se résumait en ce mot: *chute.*

—Stéphane Mallarmé

The snow is falls.

—Clark Coolidge

The streets, the falls.

The trewes, the gifts, the gavels.

The coming down, the first part.

The winters, the nights.

The grifts and runnels where the strewn leaves fleet as they leisurely spin in a lazy rotation. The slip, downstream, of debris before logging, submerging, and instantly plumbing.

The sinks and leads; the leeds and patter.

An articulation of movement (the closed vista falls into the camp of enclosure); the previous prospects; the cast of the ground — the planes away to the distance-vision's limit's strain.

The dregs of the ebb, the drain and quick suck through chameleon sand; the pervious screen of coarse sand and water-worn stones.

Into place; out of fashion; out of favor; from grace; into line.

The engraved; the names in their cases.

Heavy rain and a sudden passing.

The tributary branches and leaves.

The obligation falls to; the debts fall due; *la chance oblige.*

The flaws; the rifts and slips; the stricken faults.

The palt as blanched leaves tribute the stream from their boughs suggests a strict, unpredictable pattern.

The distributed spread, the parabola's concavity. *Le cadavre par le bras.* The dead; the wind; the free.

The randomness of dice as they fall.

Whole flocks of leaves panic at the breeze, skimming the pavement with a scraped escape.

Some trees, even unheard, unseemly, beseech.

But the puppet is graceful because its limbs are what they should be: lifeless, mere pendula, and they follow the laws of pure gravity.

The pull at the cheeks as the lips turn down — the protruding pout at the sudden conclusion.

The check of the pawl.

All the manifold catastrophes — the point of fracture or collapse; the moment of capsize; breaking waves; changes of state (melting from solids; flocs from a colloid; aggregate stages: to precipitation from high humidity, from a coating to a drop, a bead to a drip; the slip from waking to sleep); each limen of a system — follow exactly the same mathematical model.

As when, suddenly, all rivers are downstream.

The balance on the verge, from the lip, to the cusp, over the crest, down the bifurcated fold to the saddle of the buckle — at any point a plunge could fall further.

The rest depends on the sibilant difference between a fall and a kiss (*baiser*; *baisser*), on the meaningless coincidence, the chance event, the lacking logic, on an empty accident, devoid and useless — the confusion of *casus* with *cassus*.

In the same way *chance* descends from *cadere* (to fall), with its unexpected reorientation, given over to gravity, in motion beyond our control.

That random, repeated link between falling and chance finds its rendezvous again in the French *chanceler*: to falter; to look as if one's about to stumble; to tumble; to slip; (of the memory) to fail.

And yet again, in German, the sheer coincidence plays out: *Zufall* (chance); *fallen* (to drop); *Falle* (a trap, a bed — what one falls into).

(In) love; (a) sleep.

A lost night's rest is not a catastrophe.

The empty, the hollow. The dead, the free.

Compared to the person I love, the universe seems poor and empty. This universe isn't "risked" since it's not "perishable." Carnal love, because not "sheltered from thieves" or vicissitudes is greater than divine love. It risks me and the one I love. It hazards.

To aim at a mark, to wager, to guess.

We are always falling, but sometimes we forget. And because there is motion, there must be emptiness, yielding and accident. Atoms plummet though an infinite void — they rain straight down, perfectly vertical, with only occasional swerves.

As when, on some september night, in the air, you can feel the end of something and the beginning of something else: a peripeteia; a recognized crisis; a clinamen — points in the drama with a sudden reversal.

A *trama* serves to plot the path to which the warp is at any moment wefted, along the lines of termination of the web, formed by the last weft-thread driven up by they lay.

Just as each beautiful day is also a meteor (*se estrella las estrellas*).

Until the moment of collision, some portion of unforeseen motion partitions the distance remaining.

> The tea leaves, the cake crumbs — the sound of a bell, the smell of fallen leaves — the chips as they may.

With blue cærulea stewed as a potion, *catananche* (*asteraceæ*) blooms in the brew. Infusions are taken as slopes speeding sleep. The sugars dissolve; the dyes diffuse; the thyme embitters as it steeps.

The blossoming losses accrue.

Cupidone blooms from mid-june to late august — the tender perennial grown as an annual, seed-sown in soil that drains.

> Then the sepaline drop, the wither.

> Everything rinsed out, bleached pallid and spoiled.

> The achenes, the scarious bracts. The cast and the

blanched.

The nights; the made weathers; the winters.

The precarious, impending and staggered.

From the scabs to the scars to the aches.

The slid and the lanched.

The wrench of the branched clastic carpals in catch.

The scales and bracts frame bundles of stamina bound by their filaments.

The fathomed petals scroll as they dry.

Phosphates drop while anthocyanins rise.

Maple stains the sidewalk after showers; burnt-earth red remains in soaked ghost silhouettes of frozen, settled smoke.

The back and the back on; the rink of the belt.

The sifting of fells. The tymp-arch for tapping of iron and slag. The gothic drop of the fauld.

The victim to.

The vitrified refuse and calcinate cinders; the furnace soot.

The foot; the particular tread; every ambulatory moment; the other shoe.

All the lymphatics.

Each particulate in every suspension.

The spillway, the mud spew, the quicksand. The draws. The fill from the point of extraction — the drays in translation all the way to the very point of deposit.

The mudflow; the glue pour; the asphalt rundown; the endless displacements; the concrete overflow.

The outwash; the melt and the runoff; the watershed.

And then — as one's downward gaze pitches from side to side, picking out random depositions of salt crystals on the inner and outer edges — a vertiginous keel.

The sudden declivities, the vague inclinations, an inaccessible precipice; precipitates.

At the edges of the walk the slate of the paves of the path are halved. Notched, cut away at a bevel, the slabs, chipped and fit, nestle into each other with a mutual overlap.

> The total pitch and batter of the bank. The flag and the drop of diminutive bends, from the sinister chief to the dexter base.

> The sinter and leached reach of scoriated recrements, sedimented lees.

> The beleaguering leak from fothering failing.

> The further back; the so far behind.

> The forging, forgetting — the spans of the gaps of what slips from the mind.

> The indiscriminate scarp of the hills; the crest of the slopes; the cast up and cupped inner sides that envelop a ditch.

> The hollow of a vessel, bowl, or drinking vessel.

> The hollow of the waves, the breast, the depths.

A sinus trims the border with a cyma.

The seech foams the border of the bay.

A search forms the order of its finds.

Above the iris the cataract attracts a glaucal mist.

A fine spray of the drew, from the falls, scrims the vista with
   whisps.

Cascade descends straight from *cascare* (to fall), a synonym of
   cadere, from *casus* (an accident, a chance event), all miraculously
   unrelated to the Spanish *cascar* (to shatter, to break into
   pieces) — the result of an accident, from which *cask*, from
   quassere (to strike), from *cassus* (hollow, empty, devoid).

So the cask anticipates the crash from its fall, the shatter already
   before the slip, its telos in shards, in shared forms.

And then I can feel, on the tip of my tongue, the angular cut of the
   shattered word.

Chapped orange, the rolled lip of the leaf cracks to split.

The calyces shed, heralding the breeze; the seedpods shiver and
   tinder with the set.

The Danaïde heald their containers in endless unintended
   libations.

The somber coincide; the serious factionate; the somatic weights.
   The season sinks in and shadows itself in the foundering.

The ombrian curves scale probable rainfall. Statistics allays the
   uncertain.

   To cause dust to settle; to quell; to bring down or unravel.

The swell of a curtain, from irregular currents, curtails.

Hail, hastily, gavels the concrete in a rapt tattoo; dry pellets pelt the
   petals to the pave; they scatter in brief rebounding Brownian
   bounce.

   The ice as it falls; the onding, in passing.

   The span in collapse; the mermaid; the one gift.

   The stifle and puzzle: embarrassed, perplexing.

If you would have come to meet me, I would have run toward you
   on the platform, right next to the track — I would have done
   everything so as not to fall.

But the body itself opens the chasm into which it falls and falls
   away from itself — a *katabole* — projecting the ground on
   which it founds and founders in its tumble.

   The spread and the splatter; the links.

The ferruginous, interminable, frozen sound; the rink run of inlets and slews.

The terminal velocities attain; friction's equivalent of fluid drag balances.

The slow exuvial slough.

Glossed drops depend in a frozen drip from the whitewashed platform, rust leaching in spots and breaching the bleach.

The scaffold, the lattice; the framework, the catafalque.

The downward, sickling sweep of the falx, in reap.

The peduncled skull in a forward arc propels from occipital weight.

The mean part of the dura mater divides and descends.

The martelling peen.

The sickening smack of the skeletal impact.

The weight of the matter. The cut of the deck, the crack of cement, the concrete, the fact. The momentous; the met. Some sharp edge of a platform.

The whole in slow motion. A crushing blow, a heavy stroke

— the held at bay.

The cades, the *cadeaux*, the cascade.

The bailed to bade. The fated to fail.

The structures crushed to a fine granulation.

The dust to the plush, the pills to a powder; the pulver, the pollen, the dander and villi. Every last grain to the ground.

The molars, incisors and canines — the vaginal process; the jugular fossa; the mastoid — each down on the lip.

The lashes.

Type after the strike, back down to its basket — free felled as spent lovers collapsed to the bed after coitus — keys dropping like wasps in the autumn, stunned after the sting.

The vespers; the wisps; the tomentous slips; the hairs in the hollow of the back so fine they cannot mat.

The downy; the down; the pubescence.

The pinions.

The descanting frayed; the refraid; the descent of the leden;

the burden of song.

The flittered pines; the flottered pate, the pain.

Foliaceous strays in soft flutter to the lawn. The chancelled; the littered; the lanced.

Leaves weave a lace-work lattice on the grass. An intricate figure of expected, unpredictable scatter traces a persian carpet of the probable; in the strew and spread of statistical pattern, the stochastic, clastic, distributed plot postulates its own hypothesis.

Then, the compulsory crush: the pestle of steps; the must of the crumble. The dust of dried sage between fingers.

The heeled seed, spurned; the sweep of the arm over fields in cease with a supinated palm.

A wing or a leaf in catenary swing — indistinguishable in the dusk. The inevitable rush of water in its seek.

The scoria, talus and scree.

An owl feather drifts between listing stones.

The linear, persistent, acerose sting of the sudden conclusion arrives at the end of some long-held opinion.

La tige fluette; the fluid; the flood.

Those threaded sleeves that leak the pipes that link.

The sink of blood. The sag of tissue. The soak into porcelain cracks and between decaulked seamed ceramics. The pooling to contusion. The bags that hang in shadows under eyes. The lacquering stanch. The blackening scab that granulates above the pink; the reissue.

The fissures, the faulting and slips.

The chutes and flumes; the flukes.

The persistent assault of the season's caducous rebuke.

Between the seas and these tearwaters — scant difference.

Acanthus curls over itself, wrought branches fraught with verging leaves.

Carotenoids surface; anthocyanins surge.

The flourish of the cadel fades as a paraph; the signature traces apparent remains.

Harbingers harbor some crypted gifts still. Certain residuals, for some unknown reason, have lapsed as the willed are cast into receivership.

Above runnels and grifts, caduciferous boughs taper and twist;
their torsions tear the air; vine-twined arbors herald the season's
loud praise.

Wasps sklent to scent the caltrop's nectre, alighting.

Stems slender and spreading, the plants' blossoms powder under
lanceolate whorls of bracts and inflorescent umbrels.

The systyle columns sustain their close companionship; they stand
too close and yet refrain from touching.

The corrective entasis deceives. The unseen curvatures perjure,
beguile and charm.

Hair down, waving and helical from the least humidity, everything
loosened and looking so undone, she echoes: the mermaid; the
one gift; the bridges failing.

With undulate pulses medusæ sink and swell. They taper down
like ink let drop in water.

Where a drop that sinks while still suspended to the surface by
some tension attenuates, it flutters to shape medusoid vortices of
various graded forms: the threads suspend; the cupolate chute
ribbons; the little bell begins to ring.

We think of the bubbles in a liquid as rising, while forgetting that
they simply mean some other particles are falling to take their
place.

But rather than speaking of a synthesis of rising and falling one
should speak of a continuity of the aesthetic form that does
not allow itself to be disrupted by the borderlines that separate
rising from falling.

The new lover: arrived from everywhere then. The new
lover: departing everywhere hence. A spondee, a dactyl,
three trochees.

On some cool morning one finds the petals of a moth orchid
morbid in the pot.

The wasps to cold are lost.

The fever, by degrees.

The final foot drops.

The cause of to much slepynge dothe come of great graueditie in
the heed thorowe reume.

French oak, in ruin, rinses dissolution to the roots.

The rot of the cabinet, the fox of the cards.

The catalogue dorms in its own disrepair and despairs of sustaining
its index — all the references to succeeding words or groups,
now lost in a deep, or even a deadly late sleep.

The proper names; the nouns and the pronouns; the words
in their cases. The nascent; the crowned; the decided.

The hidden, defrauded, the into obscurity — the dimmed.

Shadows are the spells cast by luminence.

The rain is fell in divisions between downs.

From the cut to brushed cinnabar to desiccated yarrow the
osteomance leaves heat cracked scapula as the sortilege abandons
cast plastrons in middens.

The claster of the stones.

The parceled by lots.

The throes, the throwns.

The forecast rains — tomorrow or some other day, at
some uncertain hour. The drawn; the drained to bay. The
clouded over lower.

The roe deer fallow at the field's burnished edge dusk along the
   margin of the wood.

   The should of the derivative.

   The shied of the lanced from the hand.

   The slive of the tide from the shingle.

   The volume dropped — place lost — closed, in a doze.

   The board to the book by a cord; the single-fold scored, the
   sheaf of loose pages laid loose on the gavel.

Leaves macled, the sheets of the tome that has sunken and risen,
   that submerges and rises, buckle, unbroken, uneven: their
   crink and adhesion; their translucent wrinkles; the drains from
   the flood of the sizers' seep of asymmetrical, redistributed
   concentrates staining. The boards warp, containing the waves of
   the brittling, implant pages.

   The cast of the timber. The tumbled, autumnal, in turn.

The faltering grip of the late leaves' caducity, compulsory, gives.

   The ruins, the sluice.

The thorns and edges and yokes and ashes. The wends of the branches exposed to the wind.

Bare rocks outcrop from the treeline to the rim; ochre scrub-oak scumbles the slope; gabled firs comb a scrim above the rust-blush of dry-brush maple — intercalated birch dispersed in mustard dustings trim; green still lingers in the basin, screening the creek.

Within weeks, powder from these boughs, in periodic veils, unfurls diaphanous sheets.

For now, afternoon sun on spruce bleaches blue as a snow-coat, even in autumn.

Broom flowers waver over the swale's weep.

> The grape harvest; the cold mist; the frost. The low clouds and fog.
>
> The frim boles bled; the grim drip of the spiled.
>
> The spoiled, the ripened, the sliped.
>
> The swept, the wept, the swapped.
>
> The borrowed, the lent at accounts; the lenten and bowed.

The missed.

The plumbed.

The slumber.

Seasonal rates darken and densen.

A wake of grain eddies down the lathes.

Rain streaks stretch the length of the window, counterfeiting
    prison bars. The solemn drops unfurl and assume. Their
    carceral architecture simulates in silence.

A violence stimulates the plicature, which scars.

At minute intervals the ombrogaphic panes record the rate.

Rain doesn't form the only hyphen between sky and soil.

Lenticualted drops bead from stratified rocks.

The ground shows an interest in shadows, which cannot own it but
    are nonetheless holden.

The sleavings surface grain.

The fell of the pelt displays follicle patterns.

The palt's patter slows to a gradual halt.

The atmosphere condenses on the glass. The context presses as the day passes.

The carcels drop away along the focal plane at calculated rates.

With asynchronous hesitations the parceled droplets race, staining as they clear — along parallel tracks of sprint and stall — the record of their peers.

Rain lank along the pane incarcerates with a humid kind of solitary confinement.

Thin delicate fluting trims channeled supports.

Torqued branches make for a chancelled touting.

Shaded slaths and swales weather, their vertical planks planed with the grain. The roe shows an arrangement in a system of nesting: short stripes or streaks on the surface of the timber winnowing.

Reels of birchbark back-bending outward from the top in fibrous papyrus rinds peels. The sycamore slips to give up its plates in irregular patches of mottled, inelastic abstractions: light olive to whites gradating from greys among creamed coffee browns.

No shade from any plant ever more lovingly lovely, soft and sweet.

Élan vital laves in its visible vegetable forms: tacky dew pearls the
tops of the leaves with small droplets; pitch binds the needles of
a pine; amber tapped between bark wrinkles weeps: the bleed
before woundwood; the wondrous seep; the dark molasses sap
that traps small insects in its torpid downward drag.

The felt of the pell; the patter of the palt; the melt of the
matter; the cease of the held; the gradual halt.

The lot, the duty, the task.

The streets; the falls; the ruse.

The gins and brikes.

The plastron fractures from the stress; the plaster, in wraps, arrests;
it settles to set the break from the slip from the tripped.

The sinking church is flooded by the lake.

Abreast, aboard, astern.

The out; the off; the in with; the onto deaf ears.

The lease due; the pleats down, the lace. The pleas, the
implored, the misted gaze; the leas between rains. The

overcast smoothed against fray.

The felt.

A modest bodice gauze roughs from neck to gorge.

Draperies in paintings dispose with artful disarray.

The piping; the ribbing and rideled.

Rows crimped from the shirring cascade with a ribboning trim.

The strips and folds; the form of the fluid; the cut of
the rivel; a ridge of felled seams in their ranks; a lapped
inflorescence of ruche in its waves; the rhythmic flow of the
wove as it hangs. The intervention of a robe, arranged.

Soft satin-backed silk of crêpe-météor makes a curtaining undulate
drape.

The broken, the braked; the brocades. The stays to the
flanks.

The stoppages — blind stitched, and metered. The fate in
reserve.

A needle dropped on a floor lands between planks with predictable
play.

Calculary lots clot accountable, lacunar gaps.

>   The rasp of a thimble; a throw of the dice. Anything
>   temporal.

The slow approach of the dusk, crepuscular, precourses diminution
for this beautiful day.

>   Then the disastrous, constellated, crash of the stars.

>   The heavy stroke, the crushing blow.

The stones are dropped by the tide's retreat.

The cathedral founders (*engoutté, engloutie*), swallowed by the
billow of the lake.

>   This morning, the swale: drained, descant, decanted.

>   The plagal cadence in a long decay, with a held sustain,
>   with the tempo grave (*amabile soave più*).

>   The staves of the cade, the cadeau, the cascades.

>   The frozen sound in its endless suspension. The trust in an
>   echo.

Arches, in series, diminish down vanishing avenues, ravishing.

With only thorns adorning their bush-branches roses in lines align.

As lope the days, as leap the eaves.

The seas, with leisurely seizures, sheave laqueat, saline-sized heaves
in slack measures.

The inframince difference between oceans and tears.

The desperate sentiments and serious aches; the cake of the
sediments; certain evaporates; all of the salts.

The air to the ground. The ground to a halt. The lowest
place; the connate water; the fossil sea. The cognate,
complacent.

The abruptions of the shaling husks and failing flesh of
liquiscent fruit; occasional eggshells on grass shafts in
shards; the insides of shallow concavities nacred with glare.

A certain volume, a beautiful tension, your sweet soothing
tone. Any series of words with the same inflection.

A crystal text; a petrified shell; a stone on which reflected
light plays.

A stone from the surface of which the sun was reflected.

The play of the glare on a rock; a prisming crystal.

The light from everywhere, always obliquely.

The comfort of knowing that everything else is also beholden to laws we cannot yet explain.

Not so much a pull, perhaps, as a kind of thickening of space; the slight lessening of a glowing, slowing in its passage.

Gravity in waves, with the natural wake of a gait; the tilt and the pivot and pitch.

One consequence of a Lorentz invariance played out.

Two spheres from a tower in Pisa.

The essence of sculpture.

An alleged name for a covey of flight.

The sun to the horizon, daily, it seems.

(each beautiful day also a meteor)

Now love trying to tell us what science has always kept saying, what
all physics comes down to: everything, everywhere, falls.

About ones ears, to pieces, apart.

The far behind. The in together. The always short.

The lac of the resin.

The decident conviction.

A system's limen.

What little was left of our shed summer skin.

When casual chance is taken as causal, happenstance change is
seen as a symptom. And so the coincidence reoccurs, this time
in Greek: *symptom* comes down direct from σύμϖτωμα (chance,
accident), from ϖτωμα (a fall, a misfortune).

The love-sick, still; the sill of a sleep; the sell of the page;
the swallowed pills; the stake for a stroke as a pell.

Clamped tight to the grillwork, the rusting bell's clapper from
peals to damping retires.

Chance is defined by desire, though not necessarily every response
to desire is by chance. Anguish alone completely defines chance

and chance is what anguish regards as impossible.

The loss we cannot yet explain.

The spires drop, engulfed in aspiring mere.

All of the glass, in each antique window, flowing down slowly, miming its silicates, spreads at the pane-frame like hourglass sand.

The dust has, the silt do, the dew will, the snow must.

The glance, the glace, the face. The eyes upon, in averted blanch.

The reigns and regimes.

Not to mention: the ships, the towers, whole civilizations. Everything decadent.

The permanent home.

The saw of the beds of unballasted tumbrils; the smack of the boards on the cobbles; the tempered, the timbred.

La signature reste demeure et tombe.

The written; the set; the put. The buried; the solemn; the

given.

The serious, heavy and pregnant. A ceasing to speak.

Rain, also, punctuates the space between ground and air.

The continuous chthonic longing; the endless tug on every
elevated body.

What seems to say: *it falls*; *it shades you*.

Love acts as a kind of amnesiant, making us forget that emotion,
including its own, is completely soluble, however slowly, in time.

And more, what Orpheus hadn't remembered: the gravity of
Hades — how the earth would have pulled at her all summer,
its claw tracks scraping downward in their dermal drag; sunken
parallel staves raking the swell of her breasts and the chuff of
her hips and just barely the cusp of her shoulder — the smooth
lipid shine of stretchmarks like fine rag-paper scored with a
bonefolder.

Eurydice at the earth's core, pulled equally in all directions, relaxes
— suspended — with zero apsis.

The song of a burden; the leaden descent.

The Claude-glass-cast of the lots at dusk.

Vertebrae, vertical, turning, compressing. . . spondyls to spindles responding, rachial.

A spondee, a dactyl, three trochees.

The truce, the rifts, the gavels.

To cast for the penalty, the verdict, the judgment; the sponded arraignments.

The strips of the field thrown into divisions.

Par une chute ou par une remontée, par une glissade.

The striated bark of rues engrails the border of the park. The marbling arrangement of markings in the lignous grain radiates — nested, concentric. The gravel, in seams, sorts between slabs of cement, settling with a certain sad calculus.

The cutting from the slip.

The sleeping places. The semen; the increased risk; the cementation of the sheets.

A small shoot taken from a tree for the purpose of grafting.

The listing; the sleeting; the steeply oblique.

A crystal lace of frost, by dawn, still lattices the lawn; it melts to
    mat the plumulaceous base of feathers from a screech owl found
    among the fallen tombs and darken, before drying, the bed of
    old recumbent stones.

The roots of pines and cypress net the catacombs.

A pruinous glaze hoars the granite rims.

 The cast of the lots; the chance to be lent.

 What is left, is over, or remains; the remainder, the rest; the
    ruinous share.

 The relict land left by retreat of the sea.

 The dented margin of a sheet of water.

 The regime of the rains.

Sprigs of lavender wave, bowing and beaded.

The lands blanch detent, completely possessed.

The rain — before decidence — dashes. Its files act as syntax
    between atmosphere and earth.

(The rain in hosts is not alone).

Each meteor metes the distance of the day.

Falar shades, not far, to *fallar* (to speak; to rule in favor, or against) —
language seems to change daily, modulating with all its continuous
alterations.

> The quick crash; the coming down; the conjugate base of
> the soluble salts lends an opiate low that's so soon out of
> time.

> At the end, as they say, "out of luck," meaning, perhaps,
> *without* good fortune, or *born* from fortune, or *beyond* the
> realms in which chance and control still make sense.

> The fence posts; the pales; the ranges erratically skewed.

> The weight of the static; the plush.

In a very dry atmosphere, from early fall to late spring, film
becomes very readily charged — and in this state it attracts any
and all dust.

> Then the headlong rush; the coming to grief; the sorrowed
> regret.

> The streets, the falls, the astonished becoming.

The festival effigies burnt; the sprankling, scintillant, shift of the embers; the ashes and cinders.

The women; the skirts; the laps. The speaking, the lacking.

The rumors of the dead, the rustling.

The cries, the hawking about, the calling.

The falcons from the cliffs, waring into the gyres; the swooping of broods from the lathed escarpments, from the chipped and roughly squared crags, in a circling swarm.

Falsetto voices counterfeit, bankrupt and wanting.

The remembered scent; the density; the dance; the scant difference.

The rests and accidentals; the remains; the reminders.

The wrong hands, the sent note.

Un son de cloche, une odeur de feuilles.

The sialagogue trigger; the pavlovian pucker; the slaver.

The sleak and the rigor.

The perfect fit, tongue in groove, of tenoning ends.

The sap runs; the runes; the reans and excretions.

The ubiquitous bead of droplets that breed by absorption; then the filming: the surface's swell against tension — the ratio of dynes over area now approaching nine-hundred — and the surfactants spreading; then the wash from the let go, the let down, the overflow.

The astonishing applanate end of dispersion.

The clasping; the clapping; the paragrêle's mesh. The pelting and fell.

From the grasp; through the fingers; to the floor.

From the cymophanous surface undated, more slowly, to the rim of the deeps.

Sweet, of a fair colour, thin skin, clean faltered from haines.

The ocular scale; the Damoclean hang of anger at age.

The skin petals, *à flor de pele*; the deciduous tissues.

With each thrust, the breasts, dependent, adhere to the wave-laws of liquids.

Spine arched, head twisted back, seeking a cataglottic clasp — *baisser*; *baiser* — she pauses.

A certain amount of slip, in short, is necessary in order to obtain the thrust.

Particles of rust dye the difference — ferruginous, entropic — between the pitch of a propeller and the distance it moves through the ambient medium in one revolution.

The lachrymal, salivous, hidrotic and micturant — the colliquated, apocrine corpus in excerning fluxure diffuses in flush to an organless flow.

The catamenial charge charts calendrical measure.

The perspirant mador resudates, transuding.

> The mucinous bet against friction, the darkening swell, the dusk of the tissue.

> The soak and the sponge and the seep and the pool.

A lubricant sleves the lips down over lips.

> The slowly sapped and lactescent mucus; the mescaline

musk; the de-escalation.

The sheen of the salt-sweat, the sluicing to thighs, the
carefully powdered and carelessly pulvered now ruined or
washed-out in runs. The streaks down the dustings and
facings, the finish made spoil; foundations veering in sheets
from the stress; the silt of mascara in mirrored-out deltas;
the vistal distress of every false, sheer veneering.

Ejaculate in splatter the length of the back.

Haligraphy's minims: its strict cancellations; its blurring
and tinting and careful gradations.

The damp sheets, the creasings, the stains in their layers.

The real character of these lines is apparent when the crystalline
constitution of each grain is considered; they are not cracks, but
slips along planes of cleavage or gliding — a movement of ions,
in one layer, over another in a tensile stressed crystal.

The faulting.

The dice as they fall.

Of the tongue; from my grasp; of the pen in its writing
or copying — σφάλμα, in fact from the Greek σφάλλειν
(to err) and miraculously unconnected either to *fallan*

(German: to drop) or *fallere* (Latin: to deceive).

To miss the mark; to love you; to make a wager.

The idea of invasion, an instance of inroad, or incidence of incursion, of touch.

To risk falling again, to relapse. The for; the forward; the back on. The ruts, the grooves (*raimer, rainer*); the flood at the forest's edge, knee-deep to the girl with the orange lip.

The swollen, down-turning and bit.

The pit, the spring, the loose.

The mercury; the sudden gust; the pressure.

The young horse, stumbling.

The plunge, the plummet. Stray plumage wafting in a switchback drift.

The fled, the fledged; the fletched and flected down.

To come up, as it were, accidentally.

To fall after, of a dream: to come true. To come to.

Someone who, dreaming, says "I am dreaming", even if he speaks
   audibly in doing so, is no more right than if he said in his dream
   "I am falling", while he was in fact falling. Even if his dream
   were actually connected with the pull of the fall.

Dream may be a derivative of a *drug* (like *slip* or *fallere*: "to deceive,
   to delude, to elude").

But it is remarkable that no trace of *dréam* in this sense appears
   in Old English; yet it is clear that it must have existed, since
   the Middle English form *drêm* is regularly derived from it, and
   could come from no other source. It seems as if the prevalence
   of *dréam* 'joy, mirth, music', had caused *dréam* 'dream' to
   be avoided, at least in literature, and *swefn*, lit. 'sleep', to be
   substituted.

   Verwirren, verwunden; wondered, bewildered, in error.

   The trauma, the met: a dream of the wound.

   The web-end warped in the draft, at any moment wefted.

   Nods and somnolent drops; surfacing to paresthesiac
   shimmers.

   Quick startle of the hypnogogic twitch. And then the
   puzzle of its irresolvable uncertainty: did the dream of
   falling follow the spasmic lash — the mind's attempt to

account for its body's involuntary, myoclonic motions —
or was the stifled jerk the body's poorly paralyzed, barely
animate response to the dream?

At other times it seems our mass increases; we wake pressing into
the bed as if pushed by invisible weights, or as if there has been
some local, anomalous spike in the gravity — but perhaps we
are merely just feeling the fact that even asleep we continue to
fall.

The sleeping person is tumbled about; and when speech has been
once written down it is tumbled about.

But even when shaken accidentally, jostled at random, everything
falls into a kind of rhythmic movement, resembling dance.

The pitch of the tope.

The bottoming out.

The bottom out.

The drift, the slip — inclined, aslopen — the lull, the lay,
the bring; the slide and wax and rock.

On a hill we continually fall.

The perspective's reflection elongates inversely.

There is a cathedral that descends and a lake that rises.

Or rather: continuities of form from forms of continuous borders
conforming confound.

The summits in storm dissolve.

> The shattered; *im Schatten.*

> Askance; ashore; a chance; a cross.

> The fulled and the wrought, by rolling and pressure, with
> lees and with size — what lies, fibers open, as a text in
> compression.

In the drizzle at the bay's edge, from the fog along the shore:
rainwater equates the piles of the pier.

> Plain targets found further down, pinned to painted poles
> — the took; the once taken and no longer towing.

> The tiller, the fellahin, the towline slackening. Here the
> river's impassible, impassable downstream. The slakening
> water at rest between tides.

> To happen, befall; to fare well or fare ill; to fall as a lot or a
> portion.

The marrow, the mourn. The wan lunar decrements. The long dropped quarrels. The scruples.

From the bone to the yarrow to the thrown, wasps dart among catananche; the leaves of the Sibyl scatter in the draft — a sibilant shimmer of aspens in quiver along the bank brank, their rachides branching, reaching, embarbed.

The showers and shadows, their coincidence. A missile, a bowl, some other object; anything opaque.

The gliding sink of the shafts in flight; the stochastic try; the chased and the nocked; the bolts, parabolic, in their course. Forgetting, while calculating, that the vertical vector is parsed independently.

When the center of gravity is moved in a straight line, the limbs describe curves.

Emotion's asymptitic intensity trails, tailing — a calculus of feelings over time.

Time independent of mass.

Everything equally, leveling, falls.

The escaped; the unclasped. The held, and let slip. The no

longer held. The missed and no longer beholden. The let down; the let go; the felt.

The molten; the molted; the felled and the folden.

Felt understood as the past-tense of *fall*; *left* as the past-tense of *leaf.*

The aroused, now recumbent, back to sleep, detumescent.

The evening breeze falters.

The event comes to fall.

Heut oder morgen oder den übernächsten Tag.

To miss the mark; to love you.

To come to pass, to this.

Today or tomorrow or some other day.

In love; asleep.

Chance, obliging, choses the dancer — her stammers and tumbles, the rhythm of her steps.

The broken, the cast.

(but you didn't, but I did)

Some time, I know, I will have to let this drop.

Today, or tomorrow, or some other.

Chance is what falls due, what reaches its deadline.

The randomness of dice; the risk of desire; the slip.

For a while we forget that we are never not falling.

In love, as sleep.

Any day now and it will still be fall.

IN THE DARK WOOD

Passim: John Simpson and Edmund Weiner, editors:
   The Oxford English Dictionary (Oxford: Oxford
   University Press, 1989).
"La vie — n'est-elle pas organisation avec sentiment?" Des
   Amateurs [Volatire (François-Marie Arouet)]: *Questions
   sur L'Encyclopédie*, Vol. II (Geneva, 1774): 362.

FELDSPAR

"Feldspar" was an attempt to write a three-column text
   in which each column could be read independently,
   either of the two contiguous columns could be
   read across and down (as prose), or all three could
   be read across and down as a single conventional
   page. In every case, grammatical coherence would
   be preserved. The piece was originally composed
   letterpress, to be read on a complexly folded sheet of
   paper; as printed here, the poem elaborates all of the
   possible permutations. The original edition carried
   the following note:
"Feldspar" is a verbal landscape filtered through the
   strata of the *Oxford English Dictionary*, prospect and
   perspective changing as the weight of grammar shifts
   — one word now a noun, now a verb — the whole
   unfolding like a thin expanse of mountain meadow,

glimpsed through the trees at various elevations as one hikes along a switchback path. Grammar shears and words cleave, fractured and inflorescent, crystalline in clarity and complexity as leaves in flutter from the the dictionary's gutter: a furrow in which to browse.

THE CRYSTAL TEXT

"The moment at which a text or depiction reaches out most irresistibly…." T.J. Clark: "Phenomenality and Materiality in Cézanne," *Material Events: Paul de Man and the Afterlife of Theory*, ed. Tom Cohen et al. (Minneapolis: University of Minnesota Press, 2001): 99.

"It is always more important, more interesting, more capable…." *Cf.* "L'objet est toujours plus important, plus intéressant, plus capable (plein de droits): il n'a aucun devoir vis-à-vis de moi." Francis Ponge: *La Rage de l'expression* (Lausanne: Mermod, 1952): 11.

"The most remote and indifferent to human wishes… the most like a body the least like an organism…." Clark, "Phenomenality," 97-98.

"Some helicities of salt cause a delirium." Clark Coolidge: *Smithsonian Depositions and Subject to a Film* (New York: Vehicle Editions, 1980): 43.

"The lonely stone strips ply from ply." *Cf.* Stéphane Mallarmé, "Remémoration d'Amis belges," *Œuvres complètes* (Paris: Gallimard, 1945): 60.

"….the ceaseless weaving of uneven waves." *Cf.* Charles Reznikoff: "Aphrodite Vrania," *The Poems of Charles Reznikoff: 1918-1975*, ed. Seamus Cooney (Jaffrey: Black Sparrow, 2005): 25.

"….a will to formation, and the impossibility of forming

any other way." *Cf.* Francis Ponge: *Tome Premier: douze petits écrits* (Paris: Gallimard, 1965): 94.

"….the beauty of its own snows." *Cf.* Arthur Symons: *The Symbolist Movement in Literature* (New York: E.P. Dutton, 1918): 18-19.

"I have limited myself here to the crystal…." Clark Coolidge: *The Crystal Text* (Los Angeles: Sun & Moon, 1995): 111.

"Les pierres précieuses s'enfouissant." Arthur Rimbaud, "Après le déluge," *Œuvres complètes* (Paris: Gallimard, 1972): 122.

"Crystalline does not mean *dead.*" Clark, *op. cit.*, 98.

"Valéry's storm stirs the waves of the sea." *Cf.* Walter Benjamin: *The Arcades Project*, trans. Howard Eiland and Kevin McLaughlin (Cambridge: Harvard University Press, 1999): 453.

"But, since the crystal itself is colorless…." Gregor Maehle: *Ashtanga Yoga: Practice and Philosophy* (Novato: New World Library, 2006): 147.

"The crystal was a gift, and so it should suspend time…." *et passim. Cf.* Jacques Derrida: *Donner le temps 1. La fausse monnaie* (Paris: Galilée, 1991).

"….as one might say *a poem in prose.*" *Cf.* Marcel Duchamp: *Duchamp du signe / suivi de Notes*, ed. Michel Sanouillet and Paul Matisse (Paris: Flammarion, 2008): 63.

HALIGRAPHY

"Turning sharply toward the setting sun…." Chao Shao-an: *Bird and Autumn Leaves*, 1967 (Collection Asian Art Museum, San Francisco).

"Tout évolue aussi vers une parfaite sécheresse."
Francis Ponge: *Le Carnet du bois de pins* (Lausanne: Mermod, 1947): 29.

"The pinnacled salts." *Cf.* "Borax [...] beat down a hard path over the pinnacled salt beds of Death." Marcia Rittenhouse Wynn: *Desert Bonanza: The Story of Early Randsburg. Mojave Desert Mining Camp*, Western Lands and Waters Series, Vol. 2 (Glendale: Arthur H. Clark, 1963): 49; and "The salt pinnacles shoot forth from a brownish earth, like a quarry of marble dislocated by gunpowder. They are inexhaustible. [...] The colours of these saline glaciers are brilliant in proportion as the weather is clear." C. T. [Charles Tomlinson]: *The Natural History of Common Salt: Its Manufacture, Appearance, Uses, and Dangers in Various Parts of the World* (London: Society for Promoting Christian Knowledge, 1850): 128

"The house where I live, my life, what I write...." *Cf.* "La maison que j'habite, ma vie, ce que j'écris: je rêve que cela apparaisse de loin comme apparaissent de près ces cubes de sel gemme." André Breton: *L'Amour Fou* (Paris: Gallimard, 1937): 14.

"Slow, slow, fresh fount, keepe time." Ben Johnson: *The Fountain of Self-Love, or Cynthia's Revels* (London: Walter Burre, 1601).

"For selde it is that love alloweth." *Cf.* John Gower: *Confessio Amantis*, Book IV, l. 2282 (in *The English Works of John Gower*, Vol. I, ed. George Campbell Macaulay [London: Early English Text Society, 1970]: 362).

"Weepe you no more...." *Cf.* John Dowland: *The third and last booke of songs or aires Newly composed to sing to the lute, orpharion, or viols, and a dialogue for a base and meane lute with fiue voices to sing thereto* (London: Peter Short for Thomas Adams, 1603): XV.

"Étrangement et singulièrement...." Stéphane Mallarmé: "Pages Oubliées," *L'Art Libre: revue artistique et littéraire* I: 4 (1 February, 1872): 53.

"The snow is falls." Clark Coolidge: *Research* (Berkeley: Tuumba, 1982): [1].

Passim: Emile Littré: *Le Dictionnaire de la Langue Française* (Genève: Famot, 1977) and John Simpson and Edmund Weiner, editors: *The Oxford English Dictionary* (Oxford: Oxford University Press, 1989).

"The articulation of movement (the closed vista falls into the camp of enclosure)." Gordon Cullen: *The Concise Townscape* (New York: The Architectural Press, 1961): 106.

"La chance oblige." Jacques Derrida: *Signsponge/ Signéponge* (New York: Columbia University Press, 1984): 70.

"Le cadavre par le bras." Stéphane Mallarmé, *Un coup de dés jamais n'abolira le hasard* (Paris: Gallimard, 1993): np.

"The randomness of dice as they fall." *Cf.* "C'est l'aléa, la *chute* d'un dé." Georges Bataille: *Sur Nietzsche*, in *Œuvres complètes* (Paris: Gallimard, 1973): 85.

"The puppet is graceful because its limbs are what they should be...." Amy Knight Powell: *Depositions: Scenes from the Late Medieval Church and the Modern Museum* (Cambridge: The MIT Press, 2012): 202. *Cf.* "so sind alle übrigen Glieder, was sie sein sollen, tot, reine Pendel, und folgen dem bloßen Gesetz der Schwere." Heinrich von Kleist: "Über das Marionettentheater," *Sämtliche Werke und Briefe*, Vol. V (Leipzig: Insel-Verlag, 1912): 200.

"Manifold catastrophes [...] follow the same mathematical model." *Cf.* René Thom: *Stabilité structurelle et morphogénèse: essai d'une théorie générale des modèles* (Paris: InterEditions: 1977).

"Suddenly, all rivers are downstream." *Cf.* "De pronto, de noche, al mismo tiempo, todo río es río abajo." Julio Cortázar: *Prosa del observatorio* (Barcelona: Lumen, 1972): 31.

"Compared to the person I love...." *Cf.* "L'univers, comparé à l'être aimé, semble pauvre et vide: il n'est pas 'en jeu,' n'étant pas 'périssable.' [....] L'amour charnel, qui n'est pas 'à l'abri des voleurs,' des vicissitudes, est plus grand que l'amour divin./ Il me 'met en jeu,' met en jeu l'être aimé." Bataille: *Sur Nietzsche*, 84.

"And because there is motion, there must be emptiness...." *Cf.* Diogenes Laertes: *Lives of Eminent Philosophers*, Book X, trans. R. D. Hicks (New York: Loeb, 1925); Titus Lucretius Carus: *De Rerum Naturam*, Book II, trans. W. H. D. Rouse (New York: Loeb, 1924).

"Each beautiful day is also a meteor" [and subsequent variations]. *Cf.* "Un beau jour est aussi un météore." Francis Ponge: "La Mounine," *La rage de l'expression* (Lausanne: Mermod, 1952): 143.

"The sound of a bell, the smell of fallen leaves" [and variations]. *Cf.* "un son de cloche, une odeur de feuilles." Marcel Proust: *À la recherche du temps perdu*, Vol. I: *Du côté de Chez Swann (première partie)* (Paris: Gallimard, 1919): 242.

"Infusions are taken as slopes speeding sleep." *Cf.* "L'eau noire, l'eau lourde, l'eau mangeuse d'ombres [...] elle était là, elle fut là pour moi tout de suite, avec son odeur terreuse de vase et de racines, son sommeil dissolvant: digérant, infusant lentement les feuilles mortes qui pleuvaient des arbres d'automne [that black, heavy, shadow-eating water (…) was right there, right in front of me, with its fragrance of mud and roots, its dissolving sleep: digesting, slowly steeping the fallen leaves that would rain from autumnal trees]." Julien Gracq [Louis Poirier]: *Les Eaux étroites* (Paris: Librarie José Corti, 1977): 17-18.

"Tender perennial...." *Cf.* Leon C. Snyder: *Flowers for Northern Gardens* (Minneapolis: University of Minnesota Press, 1983): 122.

"One's downward gaze pitches from side to side...." Robert Smithson: "The Spiral Jetty," *Collected Writings of Robert Smithson*, ed. Jack Flam (Berkeley: University of California Press, 1996): 147.

"And then I can feel, on the tip of my tongue the angular cut of the shattered word." *Cf.* Jacques Derrida: "Et je sens alors, de ma langue, l'angle coupant d'un mot brisé." Jacques Derrida: "Fors," in Nicolas Abraham and Maria Torok: *Cryptonomie: le verbier de l'homme aux loup* (Paris: Flammarion, 1999): 73.

"If you would have come to meet me...." *Cf.* "J'aurais couru vers toi sur le quai, tout au bord de la voie,

j'aurais tout fait pour ne pas tomber." Jaques
Derrida: *La Carte postale: de Socrate à Freud et au-
delà* (Paris: Flammarion, 1980): 197.

"Katabole." *Cf.* Rodolphe Gasché: *Georges Bataille:
Phenomenology and Phantasmatology*, trans. Roland
Végsö (Stanford: Stanford University Press, 2012):
60-61.

"Ferruginous, interminable, frozen sound." Marcel
Proust: *Remembrance of Things Past, Vol. I: Swann's
Way*, trans. C. K. Scott Moncrieff and Terence
Kilmartin (New York: Random House, 1981): 14. *Cf.*
"son bruit ferrugineux, intarissable et glace." Proust:
Du côté, 18.

"An owl feather drifts among the listing stones" [and
subsequent variation]. *Cf.* "strigis inventae per busta
iacentia plumae." Sextus Propertius: *Elegies* Book
III, vi, l. 30; translated by W. A. Camps as "among
fallen (i.e. ruined) tombs," *Propertius: Elegies, Book
III* (Cambridge: Cambridge University Press, 1966):
81; translated by G. P. Goold as "found among
sunken tombs," 131 (Cambridge: Harvard University
Press, 1990): 273. *Tomber*, as it turns out, is entirely
unrelated to *tombe*. Falling links only by accident to
graves, despite the homophones *au tombe/ automne*.

"La tige fluette." *Cf.* "grêle, un peu glauque, simple, ou
plus tard très-rameuse; feuil. et involucres linéaires,
aigus; ombelles à 2-3 rayons dichotomes; involucelles
lancéolés [....] Tige fluette, étalée, très-rameuse;
feuil. linéaires élargies au sommet, tronquées —
échancrées, presque à 3 pointes; ombelle à 2-3
rayons; involucelles lancéolé." Auguste Mutel: *Flore
française destinée aux herborisations, ou Description
des Plantes* [....]: (Paris: Lebrault, 1836): 159.

"The sink of blood." *Cf.* Bon Iver, "Skinny Love,"
For Emma, Forever Ago (Bloomington: Jagjaguwar
[JAG115], 2008).

"Between the seas and these tearwaters — scant
difference" [and subsequent variations]. *Cf.* "Entre
l'eau des larmes et l'eau de mer il ne doit y avoir
que peu de différences." Francis Ponge: "L'Eau des
larmes," *Pièces* (Paris: Gallimard, 1971): 78. The
connection may be reinforced by the idiomatic, nearly
anagrammatic association of *larmes* (tears) and *amères*
(bitter), with its scant difference from *à mer*.

"The signature traces apparent remains." *Cf.* "La
signature reste demeure et tombe." Jacques Derrida:
Glas, Vol. I (Paris: Éditons Denoël, 1981): 6.

"Stem slender and spreading...." *Cf.* Mutel, *Flore*, 159.

"They stand too close and yet refrain from touching."
Cf. " Ils étaient comme autant d'incendies qui se
fussent épris des maisons, contentés d'exister près
d'elles sans les étreindre." André Breton: *L'Amour
Fou* (Paris: Gallimard, 1937): 79.

"Ink let drop in water [....] a drop that sinks...." *Cf.*
D'Arcy Wentworth Thompson: *On Growth and
Form* (Cambridge: Cambridge University Press,
1961): 72, *et seq.*

"The little bell begins to ring." *Ibidem*, 74. *Cf.* Marcel
Proust: *À la recherche du temps perdu*, Vol. VI: *Le côté
de Guermantes* (Paris: Gallimard, 1921): 165.

"But rather than speaking of a synthesis of rising and
falling...." Paul de Man: *Rhetoric of Romanticism*
(New York: Columbia University Press, 1984): 287.

"The new lover...." *Cf.* "Le nouvel amour [....] Arrivée
de toujours, qui t'en iras partout." Arthur Rimbaud:
"À un raison," *Œuvres*, 203.

"The cause of to much slepynge dothe come of great graueditie in the heed thorowe reume." Andrew Boorde: *Breuiary of Healthe* [...] *Book II, The Extravagantes* (London: W. Myddelton [i.e. William Middleton], 1547): folio xx, chapter 64.

"Caducity." *Cf.* "*Caduc*: qui est sur le point de tomber." Francis Ponge: "Le Carnet du bois de pins," *Rage*, 96. *Point de tomber*: about to fall, but also, equally, the absence of falling — to be on the verge or brink of falling means one still has not fallen yet.

"Rain streaks stretch the length of the window, counterfeiting prison bars" [and subsequent variations]. *Cf.* "La pluie étalant ses immenses traînées d'une vaste prison imite les barreaux." Charles Baudelaire: "Spleen," *Œuvres complètes: Les Fleurs du Mal* (Paris: Gallimard, 1918): 114.

"Rain doesn't form the only hyphen between sky and soil" [and subsequent variations]. *Cf.* "La plui ne forme pas les seuls traits d'union entre le sol et les cieux." Francis Ponge, "Végétation," *Tome Prémier: Douze petits écrits* (Paris: Gallimard: 1965): 101.

"The ground shows an interest in shadows, which cannot own it but are nonetheless holden." Cf. "Nullam verborum tenebrae et tenere synonymiam intelligens, sensus originisque cognationem vidit in tenebrae et nebula — a caligine." Josepho Furlanetto: *Totius latinitatis lexicon*, Vol. IV (Prati [Rome]: Giachetti, 1845): 290

"No shade from any plant ever more lovingly lovely, soft and sweet." *Cf.* "Ombra mai fù/ di vegetabile/ cara & amabile,/ soave più." Nicolò Minato: *Xerse: drama per musica* (Andrea Giuliani: Bologna, 1657): 1.

"The sinking church is flooded by the lake" [and

subsequent variations]. *Cf.* "Il y a une cathédrale
qui descend et un lac qui monte." Arthur Rimbaud:
"Enfance," *Illuminations,* in *Œuvres complètes* (Paris:
Éditions de Cluny, 1932): 221.

"The intervention of a robe." *Cf.* Emile Benveniste:
"La Notion de 'rythme' dans Son Expression
Linguistique," *Problèmes de linguistique générale*
(Paris: Gallimard, 1966): 333, *et passim.*

"A stone on which reflected light plays," [and
subsequent variations]. *Cf.* "Une pierre où jouait un
reflet." Proust, *Du côté,* 242.

"The comfort of knowing that everything else is
also beholden to laws we cannot yet explain."
Cf. "Letter and house seem beholden to different
physical laws, but they are melded together by a
shared gravitational force, a third reality, or field of
meanings. The letter, by contrast with the house,
isn't weighed down by the laws of nature." Patricia
Crain: *The Story of A: The Alphabetization of America
from* The New England Primer *to* The Scarlet Letter
(Stanford: Stanford University Press, 2000): 214.

"The essence of sculpture." *Cf.* "An object hung on
the wall does not confront gravity; it timidly resists
it." Robert Morris: "Notes on Sculpture: Part I,"
Artforum 4: 6 (February, 1966): 43.

"What little was left of our shed summer skin." *Cf.*
Death Cab for Cutie: "Summer Skin," *Plans*
(Seattle: Barsuk [bark47], 2005).

"La signature reste demeure et tombe." Derrida: *Glas,*
6.

"Chance is defined by desire...." *Cf.* "La chance est
définie par le désir, néanmoins toute réponse au désir
n'est pas chance./ L'angoisse seule définit tout à fait la

chance: est chance ce que l'angoisse en moi tint pour
impossible./ L'angoisse est contestation de la chance./
Mais je saissi l'angoisse à la merci d'une chance, qui
conteste et qui seule le peut le droit qu'a l'angoisse de
nous définir." Bataille: *Sur Nietzsche,* 134.

"Par une chute ou par une remontée, par une glissade"
Gilles Deleuze: "Un manifeste de moins," Carmelo
Bene and Gilles Deleuze, *Superpositions* (Paris:
Minuit, 1979): 111. *Cf.* Gilles Deleuze and Félix
Guattari: *Capitalisme et Schizophrénie II: Milles
Plateaux* (Paris: Minuit, 1980): 122.

The dented margin of a sheet of water." *Cf.* "La jolie
nappe échancrée du golfe." Honoré de Balzac:
"Seraphita," *Œuvres* Vol. XXVIII (Paris: Béthune,
1840): 19; in English in *The Works of Honoré de
Balzac,* Vol. II (Philadelphia: Avil, 1901): 6.

"Language seems to change daily." *Cf.* "La langue paraît
s'altérer tous les jours." Voltaire [François-Marie
Arouet]: *Selected Letters,* Ed. L. C. Syms (New York:
American Book Company, 1900): 164.

"In a very dry atmosphere...." Joseph H. Coenan:
"Processing of Reversal Film," *Photo Technique* 2: 12
(December, 1940): 33.

"Un son de cloche, une odeur de feuilles." Proust: *Du
côté,* 242

"Sweet, of a fair colour, thin skin, clean faltered from
haines." John Mortimer: *The Whole Art of Husbandry:
or, the Way of Managing and Improving of Land* [....],
second edition (London: Mortlock, 1708): 264.

"The real character of these lines...." Ewing and
Rosenhain: "Experiments in Micro-Metallurgy:
Effects of Strain," *Nature* 1542, Vol. 60 (1899): 67.

"The girl with the orange lip." *Cf.* "La fille à lèvre

d'orange." Rimbaud: "Enfance," *Œuvres*, 219.

"Someone who, dreaming, says...." *Cf.* Ludwig
Wittgenstein: *On Certainty* (New York: Harper
Collins, 1972): 89.

"The sleeping person is tumbled about." *Cf.* Plato;
The Republic Book V 479D; qtd. Rosamond Kent
Sprague: "Aristotle and the Metaphysics of Sleep,"
Review of Metaphysics 31: 2 (December, 1977): 231.

"When speech has been once written down it is
tumbled about." *Cf.* Plato, "Phaedrus," *The
Dialogues* Vol. II, trans. B. Jowett (New York:
Random House, 1937): 275.

"But even when shaken accidentally...." *Cf.* "Und daß
oft, auf eine bloß zufällige Weise erschüttert, das
Ganze schon in eine Art von rhythmische Bewegung
käme, die dem Tanz ähnlich wäre." von Kleist:
"Marionettentheater," 216.

"Here the river's impassible...." [*et passim* these
passages]. *Cf.* "Comme je descendais les fleuves
impassibles/ Je ne me sentis plus guidé par les
haleurs./ Des Peaux-Rouges criards les avaient pris
pour cibles,/ Les ayant cloués nus aux poteaux
de couleurs." Arthur Rimabud: "Le bateau ivre,"
Œuvres (op. cit.): 123.

"When the center of gravity is moved in a straight
line, the limbs describe curves." *Cf.* "wenn der
Schwerpunct in einer *graden Linie* bewegt wird, die
Glieder schon *Courven* beschrieben." von Kleist:
"Marionettentheater," 216.

"Heut oder morgen oder den übernächsten Tag." Hugo
von Hoffmannsthal: *Der Rosenkavelier: komödie für
musik* (Leipzig: August Pries, 1911): 144.

"Today or tomorrow or some other day." *Cf. Ibidem.*

"Chance, obliging, chooses the dancer." *Cf.* De Man,
　Rhetoric, 202.
"Chance is what falls due." *Cf.* "*Chance* est ce qui
　échoit, ce qui tombe." Bataille: *Sur Nietzsche*, 85.